Relationship Secrets For Couple

Learn how easy can be identify couple problems and solve it. Avoid Anxiety, overthinking and master anti depression techniques

Philip Steiner

TABLE OF CONTENTS

INTRODUCTION

Thank you for purchasing this book!

In this book you will find the secrets you need to solve your problems. If you are worried and anxious to be the first to start a conversation all the time you risk getting sick because your partner doesn't like you because he doesn't take the first step in communication as often as you do. Anxiety builds up and gains momentum. Force your partner to communicate with you by contacting you a couple of times until you feel reassured knowing that he will make an effort. This test allows you to challenge your anxious, irrational belief that they won't reach you first. This, however, is not a healthy strategy. Addressing the root cause of anxiety and regaining confidence is the best way to overcome anxiety disorder and leave you with a free and joyful life.

Now I leave you to your reading, and I am sure you will find answers to your questions.

Enjoy!

CHAPTER 1 - Toxic Love in Relationship

Perhaps one of the more challenging aspects of codependent tendencies is the tendency to soak up other people's distress. When you do not have good boundaries to safeguard your emotions, you end up making other people's problems your own. This effectively leads you to a codependent situation where you cannot separate yourself from the other person.

Such toxic relationships bring out the worst in you because the other person knows exactly what buttons to push to get you to toe the line. You will find yourself often doing things you would otherwise never consider doing just to keep the other person happy. This dysfunction, if left unchecked, becomes a self-repeating cycle that takes over your life.

Toxic relationships poison you from the inside out. In extreme cases, they may even drive you to coping mechanisms such as addictions to help you process your unresolved issues. This potential for self-harm is one reason why freeing yourself from codependency requires that you eliminate any toxic relationships from your life.

Whether you are dealing with a narcissist who thrives on attention and being the center of the universe or with more covert manipulators, the damage to your self-esteem is hard to repair. Toxic people will come in many different shapes and forms, and you need to identify them by their characteristics.

Here are some warning signs that you need to be on the lookout to identify toxic people and weed them out:

- They like to control you
- They like to shift blame and never take responsibility for their actions
- They are overly critical and always trying to find fault
- They use threats and intimidation to manipulate you.
- They try to gain sympathy by playing
- They are always complaining
- They often use emotional abuse to make you feel worthless.

Perhaps the most toxic relationship for a codependent is one with a narcissist. Narcissists have no consideration or interest in other people's feelings or needs. When it comes to empathy and compassion, the narcissist is the polar opposite of the codependent.

Here are the classic signs that point to a narcissistic personality:

- They lack empathy and never try to meet your needs
- They manipulate you to get what they want
- They expect you to cater to their every need and whim without question
- They demand to have the best of everything
- They are continually making you feel inferior
- They have a compulsive need to be the center of attention.

Tips for Freeing Yourself from Toxic Relationships

1) Build Boundaries

Identify your limits and do not compromise on your boundaries. Be very clear on what is and isn't acceptable. Always be ready to enforce the consequence of the other person crossing your boundaries. This means you should be ready to permanently cut off ties with this person if they are unwilling to change.

2) Stop Taking Responsibility for Other People's Problems.

The only person whose happiness you are responsible for is you. Stop trying to fix other people's problems. Never feel obligated to rescue or support someone unwilling to take responsibility for their actions.

By trying to fix the other person's problems, you become an enabler and promote dysfunction and codependence in the relationship. People tend to become more conscientious when they know that they will be responsible for the consequences of their actions.

3) Discover Your Triggers

Identify the triggers that make you vulnerable to manipulation. Whether you have unresolved issues with guilt, blame, or shame, know what your triggers are. Be vigilant around anyone trying to use these triggers against you. For instance, someone trying to guilt you into doing something you do not want is exploiting your guilt issues.

4) Build Your Emotional Intelligence

Emotional intelligence enables you to manage your emotions effectively. It allows you to stop being reactive to other people and have more control over your behavior and feelings.

Emotional intelligence also increases your social awareness and the ability to recognize other people's motives. This makes it easier for you to spot manipulators and energy vampires and give them a wide berth.

5) Find Safety and Security in Yourself

When you are secure in yourself, you no longer feel the need to be validated or approved by others. This leaves you free to make decisions based on your needs. Freedom from the need for validation also means that you no longer have to please others to feel loved or accepted. This frees you up to be true to yourself without fretting about other people's opinions.

6) Surround Yourself with Positive People

When you build healthy relationships, you will be less likely to get back into dysfunctional relationships. Focus on making new emotional connections with people who share your values. A good relationship will help you get over a bad one that much faster. It will also give you a chance to experience what a good relationship should be.

CHAPTER 2 - How to Build Self Esteem and Love for Yourself?

Let's talk about trust in yourself, and in particular, I want to reveal three secrets that will help you regain self-esteem.

Yes, because self-esteem is not something you never had. I think we naturally believe in ourselves and have faith in our abilities. I'll explain the three secrets to understand how to believe in yourself and increase self-esteem. The problem arises when we begin to let the events of life or others' judgment in a thousand forms affect us and lose sight of our real value.

Let's start now. We have an important achievement to make!

Regaining Self-Esteem: 3 Simple Free Things Will Make A Difference!

I've read dozens of journals on self-esteem, self-confidence, personal growth. Honestly, I hardly ever read the right answer to the question you are asking yourself now: how to regain self-esteem and believe in myself or myself?

All Negative Emotions Come from Fear

Fear is the basis of every negative emotion, and it is the one we feel most often, without perhaps recognizing it.

Secret 1: Don't Listen to the Judgment of Others

The fact of the matter is that we are very dependent on the judgment of others.

Do the people around you believe in you?

Or do they think that you will not be able to achieve individual results? Do people think you're an idiot? It doesn't change your self-esteem. Do they think you are a wonderful person? That doesn't count for your self-esteem either.

Think about it. The evaluation of others does not matter. Self-esteem is your judgment of yourself or yourself, not that of others. The trouble is, if those around you don't believe in you, you most likely end up believing them more than you do or yourself.

This is always wrong.

First of all, therefore, do not listen to the things that others think of us. Honestly, this applies to anyone: it could be your mentor, your father or your mother, your partner, a child, best friends, professors, or teachers of any kind.

Never believe someone who doesn't believe in you. He's wrong, and you'll end up wrong too! Start deciding what you are worth and do not care, but not at all, about what others think. Take their ideas and their judgments as mere personal opinions (they are nothing else!) And decide if they are accurate and to what extent, or if they are false. This also applies if the opinion is of the President of the Republic, the most crucial psychologist in the world, or your favorite singer.

Does not matter

And your results don't matter either. Are you unemployed, or unemployed, and have a mountain of debt? It doesn't change your self-esteem. Do you have a villa in each region? It doesn't matter to your self-esteem. Take a good look at this passage: your self-esteem is about your worth, not what you got. Do you think that if you are worth you getting something and not worth you get nothing? Imagine that you do everything well, work carefully, be precise and do everything right.

But people don't like what you've done, and your job has branded a failure. Even though it was perfect, you didn't get the success you expected. Results and personal worth are different and often very distant from each other. Don't consider what you get. Think about what you do, how you do it; consider what you can do.

You must learn to separate the results, which are conditioned by a tide of factors beyond your control, from you, from your value. Focus on what you can do. Are you wrong? We all do it. Think about how to improve.

What do you believe in? This is the fundamental question. Do you know what it means to believe in something?

Thinking it is correct, confident, safe

You will begin to believe in yourself when you think that your potential is authentic, confident, and sure, what you are. The question is whether you think you are "worth" or not.

But be careful, because this judgment is often affected by comparison!

Are you capable of living a happy life? A few minutes and ten questions will allow you to understand that you can live a joyful life if today.

Secret Number 2: How to Have Confidence in Yourself by Eliminating All Confrontation with Others

Here's how to believe in yourself: by stopping to compare yourself with others or with individual results that, always for the choice of others, we think we have to achieve. The point is to not always look out the window, whether you are better or worse.

If you want to believe in yourself, you have to start believing that you are unique, memorable, fantastic, or fantastic. Often the main problem in the comparison is the physical appearance. When we don't like our body, when we find our appearance unpleasant, we often devalue ourselves and have low self-esteem. Other times the problem is represented by work: not having one, at a certain age, or not being able to change the current one, perhaps considered unpleasant and humiliating, are often the cause of a low self-evaluation.

Many other times, it is success in a broad sense: self-esteem is negatively conditioned by having achieved an inevitable result, by the inability to have established standards of a certain level. In sports, professional, or even personal, our self-esteem often suffers from our ability to achieve what we should. Comparison is always useless: if to esteem me, I have to be attractive, if I must have found a particular job or have a house of absolute value if I must have achieved specific results and successes, the problem is never low self-esteem, but the inability to realize what matters in our eyes.

Be accepted and approved by others. If I am ugly, this is a problem when someone might mistreat me for my appearance (I am rejected by the people I court, for example). If I don't work, the self-esteem problem is only because others may see this situation as a sign of my inability and failure. If I don't win a tender, the problem arises only from clear and imposed social expectations if I don't get a promotion.

People Confuse Self-Esteem with Approval.

We compare ourselves with others because we know that if we are like all of them, we will be approved too.

The rule of self-esteem, the main one, says that we must, first of all, get rid of any dependence on the opinion of others. Aesthetic canons, success, prestige, and power are all parameters that others have established that we have accepted and decided whether we are worth it. Fortunately, in reality, our value is unchanged, although we may not estimate ourselves positively.

There is only one way to strengthen self-esteem: to realize that we always associate our value with others' judgment. Only by stopping to compare ourselves with them can we begin to live our life esteeming ourselves positively.

There are no other ways or shortcuts of any kind: if we continue to give importance to the opinion of people, whoever they are, we will never be able to have healthy self-esteem. We may meet their favor and appreciate our worth, but it won't be true self-esteem. Based on the comparison, it will not be reliable security, but only our adjustment to others' expectations, expectations destined to change, and with them, our security. There will always be someone faster, stronger, or smarter than you. This is not the way.

You are unique. From here, you have to start, also because of the third secret.

Secret Number 3: How to Regain Self-Esteem Knowing That You Are Worth Because You Can, Not for What You Do

Wait, I don't want you to delude yourself that you are an artist when you scribble on paper like a 4-year-old. The point is that believing in himself the same has nothing to do with what you do or have done.

Can you paint? Good, I am happy for you.

I don't know how to do it, but I believe in myself, and I don't think I'm inferior to Picasso or other painters.

Here's how to regain self-esteem: learning to recognize your potential. I tell you in no uncertain terms: don't care if you have won many trophies, have won a few, or have lost them all.

It doesn't count; it doesn't help. You can win them. Start with self-confidence. Ask yourself: How does a person have to behave for me to trust them? Write what he should do or say, what attitude would make you trust a person. Just think of someone you would give your house keys to, or lend your car or something valuable.

What characteristics make you give this confidence? You delegate essential things to some people, but not to others. For what reason? What's in them that inspires you so much? For example, if you trust those who are honest, start acting honestly. Trust and self-esteem are closely linked. You don't have to imitate this person, but develop the qualities you value and value.

Remember: self-esteem does not grow if others approve or accept you. It is your only thing; it depends on what you think about yourself.

And it doesn't matter what has happened so far, whether you've brought out your qualities or not.

You may have made mistakes so far, but already today, you may not make them anymore; it depends only on you.

Peruse this sonnet. I like it:

If you believe you're outside of what might be expected, you will be,

If you figure you don't have a clue how to dare, you won't dare.

On the off chance that you need to win yet figure you can't,

It is practically certain that you will fall flat

On the off chance that you envision losing, you have just lost,

Since on the planet, the facts demonstrate that

Achievement starts with the desire of the person,

It's in his psyche

On the off chance that you trust you are outmatched, you are.

To rise, you should reach skyward,

You must make certain of yourself first

To have the option to win a prize.

Human rights don't generally grin

To the most grounded or quickest man.

Sooner or after, the triumphant man

He will be the person who figures he can win.

You can win.

If you don't confide in yourself, nobody else will have it in your place.

Self-Confidence

You may have all the tools you need to accomplish your goals, but you will fail if you don't believe in yourself. I don't know how many times I've read this sentence in personal growth manuals and do you know what I thought each time? "What para-asses this para-gurus! In the end, if the strategies they propose don't work, it's always my fault that I didn't believe it enough! So, everyone is good!" Yet, the link that exists between success and self-confidence is undeniable.

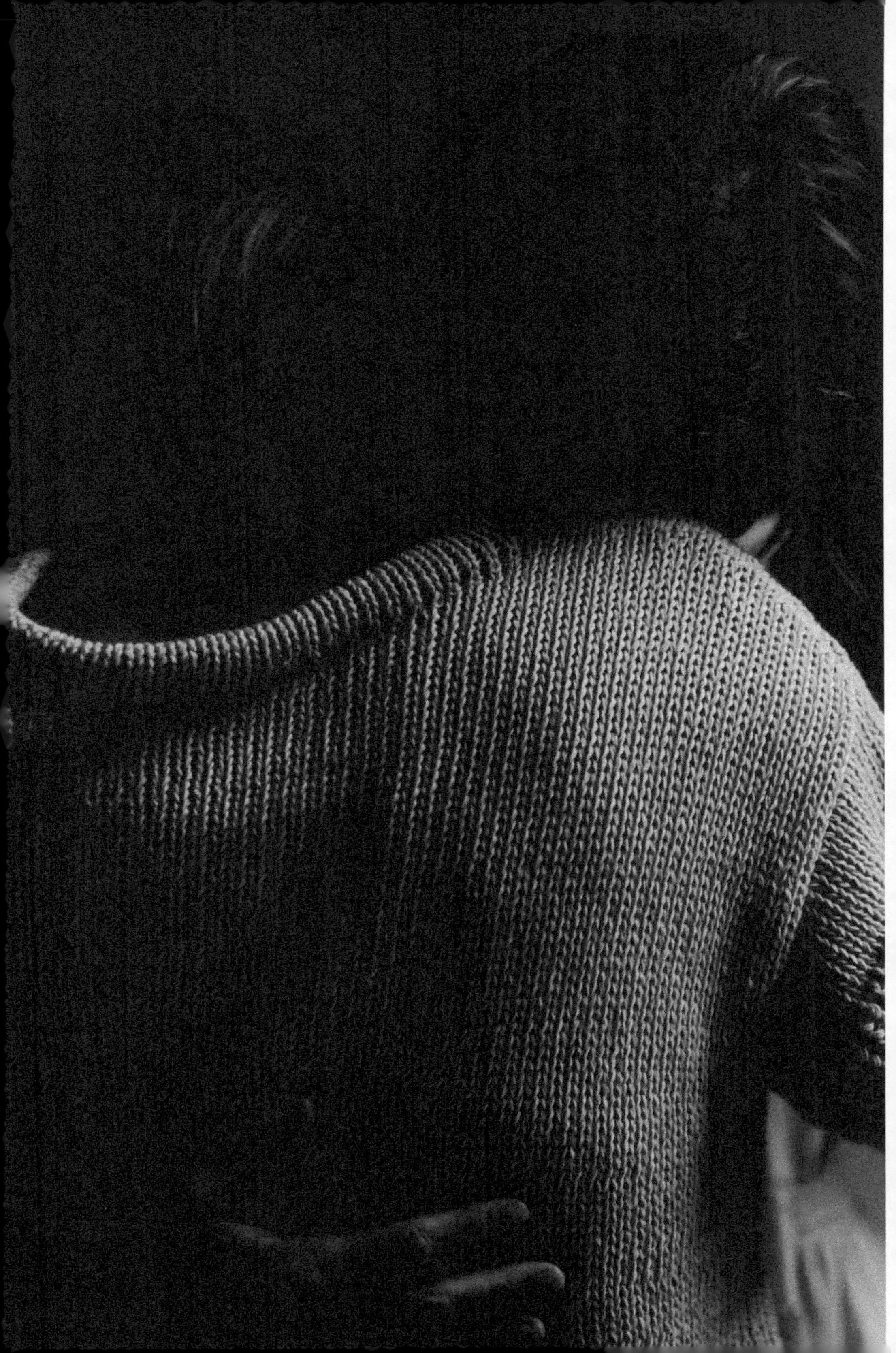

CHAPTER 3 - Strategies of Self-Control and Emotional Dependence

Emotional dependence has some costumes that make them attractive. Forms that make us fall into it, to experience its unpleasant consequences after.

Emotional dependence is one of the most frequent reasons for consultation, although clients or patients do not think in principle that this may be the reason. Although we do not know if this prevalence is real since the data is based on the frequency with which they go to the clinic, the prevalence is higher in women.

When a patient suffers from emotional dependence, the psychologist does not usually suspect him since he can hear how the patient verbalizes that "he loves his partner too much," or "he will change over time when he becomes aware."

Although the person's needs are relegated to a second, third, or fourth level, the primary objective is that your partner does not despise you or is not absent from your side.

In this sense, the emotional dependent can abandon projects that are important to him, neglecting other people, spending excessive amounts of money on gifts, or even setting limits on disrespect or humiliation on his partner's part.

Some people go so far with their emotional dependence that they throw away their whole lives, this problem becoming generalized to their work, their family, or their social environment.

We can imagine how these people's self-esteem is when they put their partner far above themselves, even if it hurts them. What happens is that there is an unresolved emotional lack that they try to fill with another person's fleeting affection.

For this reason, abandonment is so essential since it would mean becoming orphans of love or affection, something that they lack alone.

How Far Can Emotional Dependence Go?

When I explain emotional dependence, I usually draw a "puppet" running behind a heart with a hole in the center of his body—as if they were missing a piece. The hole, which also has a heart shape, can only be filled with Self-esteem, that is, with the heart that the patient places himself.

The clerk does not know this and thinks that running after a heart outside is the solution to his problem. And run, run, and don't stop running, for days, months, even decades. What is the result of this demanding career? The only consequence that our "puppet" obtains is precisely exhaustion.

The heart is not reached, and if it is reached and we place it in our hollow, it does not help us. It is as if it is not our size. And the question that is essential to understand is that no heart will fit.

The only heart that can serve us, as we have said, is the one we give ourselves. And in this sense, power is not outside but born from within.

But, if we don't know this, the result is that we can go very far on that expedition. We can lose our friends by leaving them to avoid rejection from our partner; we can sabotage our values, tastes, hobbies to satisfy the other person. We can abandon jobs, trips, and exciting projects because we don't want to leave our partners, which means their loss. We can even become jealous and try to control everything the other does, with the suffering that entails an unfortunate result.

What can we start doing to avoid falling into this trap?

Self-Control Strategies in Emotional Dependence

The techniques from the psychological point of view that we can carry out to gain self-control in an emotional relationship have to be aimed at managing our most passionate and entrenched impulses.

Emotionally dependent people, as with other agencies, know that their way of acting hurts them, but they cannot stop doing so because their "emotional GPS" helps guide their actions.

It is difficult to break the dependent habit, but after all, it is only about that: a habit or a pattern learned and can be unlearned with determination.

Some ways to do this unlearning are:

When you type a text message to your partner or ex-partner as an attempt to control, either by jealousy or by knowing what he thinks or what he is doing, you should write that same message on a blank page. In this way, you gain time—the emotion lowers its intensity in a few minutes—and you also force yourself to get it out of your mind before retyping it on your mobile.

This simple exercise can create "reactivity," which is an advantage as it can inhibit you from finally doing the action.

Try to practice zero contact. If the relationship is over and you're still hooked, try reducing the actual connection to zero. Remove them from all social networks, avoid meeting friends in common or frequent places where you can run into one another.

If you feel the urge to go to his house, get close to talk to him, etc., do a contrary behavior. If you have to take the car and drive on a specific road to go to his home, deviate to another alternative way that forces you to make many turns to reach your primary destination. As in the rest of the strategies, this will allow you to save time and think more rationally.

Think about what you will get by following your impulses. Will he come back to you? Will you get him to explain to you, as you want, why he is no longer by your side? Will you get him back with you? Do you want to return with him? If, after all the questions, you conclude that you are not going to come to anything other than an argument, fatigue, or irritation that you could have saved yourself, reconsider if you still want to follow your instincts.

Make a reminder card. When you are emotionally calm, write a reminder card that you always have to carry with you to access it. You have to write sentences that help you not take the step to the dark side when you are too emotional. They have to be phrases that come to you and serve you. An example could be: «You already have experience and know that acting in this way only ends up hurting you. Isn't that a good reason to keep the effort to control your impulses? »

Self-control in emotional dependence is difficult to acquire. It requires constant work, and, even so, nobody is immune. We have to know that falls or relapses are part of the process and continue to persevere.

Little by little, with practice, we will gain self-esteem and stop getting involved in relationships based on dependence to generate and maintain healthy, smooth, and fluid relationships.

Self-esteem and emotional dependence: communicating vessels

We are social creatures. We like to please and impart things to other people. However, would this be able to the requirement for endorsement be unsafe to us? Here is one of the keys to passionate reliance. Do you need to like everybody or simply those imperative to you? Who are the pertinent individuals in your day-to-day existence? Do they need to affirm all that you do?

I welcome you to ask yourself these inquiries and attempt to respond to them. It is something special to be clear about what you need to do and realize that you might want your friends and family to support it and another to feel that if everybody doesn't adore you, things are not justified, despite the potential benefits ... The distinction, however inconspicuous, is as yet fundamental. Peruse on to figure out how this impacts your prosperity!

What Is an Emotional Dependency?

Individuals with passionate reliance unreasonably need the warmth, consideration, and endorsement of others. They feel a silly dread of depression and deserting, which will make them more subordinate in their relational connections. Likewise, they have a powerful urge for selectiveness and report that they couldn't envision existence without their accomplice.

In this manner, they present a relentless example of feelings that they can't fulfill themselves, so they plan to cover them by setting up wrong binds with others. They create parasitic and topsy-turvy connections, complete demonstrations, everything equal, and conditions that legitimize with a solitary reason: that the relationship doesn't end.

What's more, not just that. They long for sentiments of security and love with such force that they search for it in the other individual so that they drop themselves, paying little mind to the nature of the relationship to look after it. Along these lines, they build up extreme and temperamental connections as opposed to more advantageous ones. We, as a whole, prefer to feel cherished. However... we are not ready to do anything to get it.

How Does Emotional Dependence Influence Psychological Distress?

The issue of being genuinely needy—in overabundance—on others is that, on the off chance that they don't get the consideration or the unreasonable love we need, there are stupid questions about our value and the gratefulness that others have for us, which will impact our confidence and the feelings we feel.

In this manner, show up sentiments of dismissal, refusal, and surrender. Along these lines, trouble is available too seriously, prompting us to enter an endless loop of an emotional void and ongoing disappointment. It is hard to get out: despondency.

However, not just that, the dread of being separated from everyone else that leads individuals to dodge depression successfully makes restless indications increment. The individual foresees this incident's chance, which makes him anxious and participates in harmful passionate connections.

Against Passionate Reliance: Confidence

As you can envision, individuals with passionate reliance have low confidence and see themselves adversely. Once more, this leads to a more noteworthy need to look for help and friendship in others. All in all, to be well, they need others to be well with that person.

The reality is that the only person we spend our entire lives with is ourselves. Therefore, it is essential to base our well-being on seeking our approval and not that of everyone else.

What do I mean by this? That the first person we try to please with what we do must be ourselves.

But what else can we do to like ourselves more? A straightforward exercise would be to look every day for something that has made us feel good, both physically and psychologically. In the beginning, it is a task that will cost us since we are not accustomed to flattering ourselves, but in the long run, we will foster positive affection with our person. In this way, we will reduce pathological emotional dependence. Love yourself!

CHAPTER 4 - When Does Your Codependent Relationship End?

It is easy to become mutually dependent in a narcissist relationship, regardless of whether you were sure previously. It can generally be depleting to need to oblige their requirements for consideration. You may ask why that is, the reason anybody would let the other individual control you as though you were a manikin. It isn't deliberate, that is, without a doubt. The narcissist will give their accomplice love and consideration regarding whether they are also narcissistic or acknowledge that much consideration. Presently, we as people can't avoid the pleasantness of friendship that somebody is giving us.

When it comes to relationships, especially with a narcissist, you are expected to make them happy and to cheer for them no matter what. You are expected to be there to support them and to help them in whatever they need help. They expect you to be with them night and day and that you are the one who will keep their spirits high. However, is it possible to rely on one person about everything?

The step you can make is to start making decisions on your own. These essential things matter both to you and your partner, and these should be made together. However, if you are a codependent person, you will wait for your partner to decide on everything instead of you. If you gain control over at least the smallest things, it will be considered excellent progress.

Codependent persons are usually wholly dependent on other people's will and decisions. Therefore, you need to start making small decisions and gradually move on to some bigger ones. So, what if you make a mistake? Everyone else makes mistakes, you need to learn from them, and move on. Even if you do make a wrong decision, usually there is enough time to fix it. If you do not fix it, it will serve as an excellent lesson for the future. You will know that you need to consider some other things when decision making. These things will depend on what you are deciding on. However, leave those big decisions for together decision making. It is better to discuss your partner's pros and cons than make a massive mistake that a narcissist will most likely never forget. Thus, you should wait for you both to decide.

Learn how to stabilize without anyone else's help. When you are codependent, it may seem like you have no idea how to calm down and look at things cool headedly. You need to try different techniques and find the one that works best for you.

You have to have in mind that you and your partner may not have the same opinions on all topics. And that is okay. There are no two persons that share the same opinions and views on everything. Diversity is good. If you live with a narcissist, they might try to make you think like them. They will insist on doing things their way.

When it comes to goals, it is a great thing to have common goals with your partner. Those goals may not be the same as what you have set before your life with your partner. It will help you remember what your aims are. You may even change your mind about some goals over time, and that is okay. People change, so should their goals. If those goals do not match your partner's, you may get into a conflict.

However, you should compromise when those goals matter to both of you, and you should do it equally. If you are willing to give up on the part of your lifetime dream, then they should too. You should not allow a narcissist to control you so much that you do not even have dreams anymore. Having goals and dreams drives us forward, and no one should ever be able to ruin them. We must not allow anyone to do that. This is where setting boundaries comes in hand. You will tell them that you have other plans and that they do not coincide with theirs. You may compromise, but do strive to accomplish your biggest dreams.

The final step in getting more independence is to enjoy your life. It is too short to waste it on pleasing others who will probably not even notice the hard work you are putting in to please them.

CHAPTER 5 - Find the Pleasure

Identifying a codependent relationship is tricky. It is often disguised in any individual's willingness to adapt to other people's needs.

People in general, consciously or unconsciously assign all the people in their lives a role to assume. They then deal with these people based on what they think these people want from them. In essence, it's like presenting a puppet show of your life. You may not realize it, but you are orchestrating the whole show based on what you conceptualize in your head.

Some people are somewhat oblivious of the "roles" they assume, some seem to be detached, and others run along the lines of being codependent. To put an end to or overcome a codependent relationship, you need to recognize a person who "suffers" from codependency.

You will find in the succeeding paragraphs some of the most common codependent "roles." Do not be surprised if you recognized yourself in more than one. You will also find some strategies to change the script, so that nobody becomes the codependent party.

Martyr

For martyrs, suffering is virtuous. They are happy when they were able to put the needs of their loved ones ahead of their own. They are the ones who would be the first one to take on an extra project and always the last person to leave the office. They would pick up the tab voluntarily even if they are broke. Recognize the signs? It might have been the concept that your parents and your religious belief have instilled in you.

The Issue: You might not have realized it yet, but when sacrifice is your norm when it comes to relationships with loved ones, friends, and colleagues, you tend to neglect your own needs to be loved and cared for. While these are the things that you are hoping to get by giving more than you can give, chances are your efforts can backfire. When you don't get what you want from the relationship, you'll begin to resent these very same people to whom you've extended your help.

How to Overcome: Begin to Care for Yourself?

You must understand the difference between self-care and selfishness. You have to realize that you are not selfish if you opt to leave the office on time or if you want to go out with friends once in a while. It isn't rude if you ask to split the bill if you can't afford to shoulder everything. You have to begin to care for yourself because no one else will. Ernest Hemingway, an American author, and journalist, once said, "My health is the main capital I have, and I want to administer it intelligently." If we don't have our health, we have nothing left to give. It's similar to the idea of how to respond to an emergency in a plane crash: put on your oxygen mask first before helping others, or else you are no help to either of you.

Savior

A savior takes pride in being the one to solve all conflicts. He is the one who's always there to lend money when a friend needs it, even if he is equally broke.

The Issue: There is no denying that everyone does need help sometimes, and it is not harmful to help. However, if you feel it is your mission to be the one to give comfort to others, even to the point of creating discomfort on your part, it is not healthy. You are telling the people you've helped that they are hopeless without you. You teach them to become overly dependent on you. As a result, you've created a relational dynamic that will continuously suck energy, time, and resources out of you. People can learn to take advantage of this. They can even manipulate you to get what they want. When people get used to you being their savior, they quickly react when they don't perform that role in their life.

How to Overcome: Empower?

It is always a good thing to help; it's a win-win situation because you feel good when you can help. However, you have to examine your real purpose for helping other people. It is also important to analyze if it is also doing them good. Being there for them is one thing, but preventing them from being self-reliant is another. There are people whom you have helped once who come in for another and then another until they are dependent on you that they do nothing to improve their situation. It's not rude to occasionally say "no." When you save people from their problems, you may be robbing them of a lesson that they need to learn for themselves. If you feel that helping other people is the only time that you are needed and loved, then you are not in a healthy relationship at all.

Adviser

Are you an adviser? You probably can look into someone else's problems and offer solutions and advice. The adviser is not too good a listener, though.

The Issue: People come to you because you give good advice. You feel happy because they continuously come to you to hear what you have to say. You assume that they lack self-esteem even to solve their problems. In reality, though, advisers are the ones who are insecure, and they feel needed when people come to them. They are the ones who lack self-esteem. They want to feel in charge and in control, and the only way they can do that is to tell someone what they have to do.

How to Overcome: Set Boundaries?

If someone comes to you and pours their heart out, try to listen to them for a change. Just by listening, you can help your friend or your loved one. You don't have to tell them what to do. Let them make the decision themselves. Let them see for themselves the perfect solution to their problems. You can give them your two cents' worth, but only after you have listened to them and do not tell them what to do. Give them options and then let them decide. Do not tell them outright that they have to do this or that. Respect their judgment; be a friend, and just listen.

Ultimately, people need to come to their conclusions about their problems.

People Pleaser

The people pleaser is the one who always volunteers to organize something for the community. They are the ones who volunteer to fix everything. They bask in the glory of being "appreciated" for their hard work in initiating gatherings, parties, and fund drives.

The Issue: It is not a problem if you are the go-to person when it comes to social gatherings, but it becomes a problem when you begin to feel that doing so becomes a chore, yet you cannot say "no" because you don't want them to stop liking you. People-pleasing is passive manipulation. You do things for other people because you can get something from them.

How to Overcome: Learn to Say No

It is not your loss if you say "no." The following time the office needs a volunteer, think twice before stepping up to do the task. Analyze if people are indeed going to dislike you if you didn't volunteer. Are you up for another task? Don't you have other important things to do at home? Learn to say "no" not because you don't want to do it but because you need to do other more important things. There is always time for everything. Besides, the world won't fall apart if you say "no." You can be replaced. People are capable of finding other people to help.

The Person Who Says "Yes" All the Time

Have you ever been in a situation when you had to say "yes" when you wanted to say "no?" Did you resent your action? A person who says "yes" all the time is one who keeps his discomfort to himself.

You can't tell your friends what you feel for fear of offending them. You can tell your partner that you are upset because you didn't want to start a fight.

The Issue: A healthy relationship is one in which both parties or a group of friends are in total honesty with each other. If you avoid conflicts, you say "yes" when you say "no," there is a disconnect somewhere in the honesty department there.

In the office, there is something that you are uncomfortable with, but you are too afraid to tell your boss for fear that you might lose your job. You are afraid to trigger an argument with your partner because you fear that they might leave you.

So, you hide the feelings inside. When this happens, you might end up resenting them and eventually ruin your relationships.

How to Overcome: Be Honest

If you don't speak up, you will not resolve anything. Your partner might not be aware that there is a problem already until it blows up in your face. It takes courage to tell the truth, but it is liberating. You can tell the truth without hurting someone else's feelings. Talking about a problem doesn't always equate to creating conflicts; this is just the healthier way of bringing up unresolved issues to find solutions.

Did you identify yourself in any of these? You were able to hurdle the first step to making changes in your life: awareness of the "problem." Acceptance that there is a problem is critical in making improvements.

CHAPTER 6 - Welcome to Your Real You

The actual act of leaving can be terrifying. It can feel as though you are planning a murder or leaping over the edge of the unknown. Breakups are a naturally turbulent experience, and this is especially true when they involve trauma. Victims of emotional and physical abuse have been trained to accept and justify their behavior and the rest of the world. Lying to concerned friends and family to protect your abuser's image after public fights; there is a lot of P.R. and damage control that goes into these types of relationships.

Trauma bonding is the glue that holds victims to their abuser. Comfort is something that is sought only from your relationship partner. There is even this aching anticipation that you are going to have to listen to hordes of ignorant and well-meaning people tell you that they would never let themselves enter into an abusive relationship as if your partner had a giant label on their forehead when you met. A label that you gleefully chose to ignore.

Re-Establish Support Systems

In relationships with both narcissists and codependents, there is a drive toward isolation.

The goals are different, but the results are the same. A narcissist has systematically cut away all of your friends and family, keeping everyone at arm's length.

If you have been subject to these restrictions on your personal life, it is time to begin quietly mending the bridges that your partner has burned for you. Call your closest contacts from before the relationship, including your family. It may feel as though you have been shrugged off, but I promise that people still care about you and your wellbeing.

After you have reestablished the connections, it is time to fill them in on your relationship's reality, a reality that you have likely hidden for a long time. You must find help through the coming weeks. You may also need a ride if your partner has taken control of your transportation needs.

How Could You Stay?

It is so easy to save under the pressure of doubt and guilt. There are so many conflicting emotions that surface when you are contemplating leaving an abusive partner. Your younger self has always believed that you could never be the type of person to be sucked into a relationship plagued with abuse. It is so easy to judge from the outside, a concept that you have probably become intimately familiar with. You know that others will wonder why you stayed when things were so bad, so violent. Only you know the truth. It never looks the same from the inside. It isn't so easy to let go of everything that you know. This misery is misery, but it is comfortable. You have become accustomed to being treated as though you are worthless. A familiar sadness can be less frightening than the unknown.

No one will know how easy it is to lose yourself in someone else until it is happening to them. You can feel a bit like the heroine or hero in a teen romance movie. Someone with charm, charisma, and confidence sees you for the person that you are. They are falling in love with you and quickly. This person is everything that you have ever wanted in a partner.

They are so much more relaxed than you feel like you are. They are so much better than you feel like you deserve. They speak with authority and are unapologetically invested in you.

It can be dizzying. It can feel as though all those sappy romantic daydreams are coming true, all at once.

Before you even realize that it has happened, you are swept up in their world. You have changed so much about yourself, little by little. Friends are beginning to worry about you, but you are so deliriously in love that you ignore their words. Now and then, your partner becomes angry. They shatter your world with their words, but then they are there to pick up the pieces and comfort you until the pain disappears again. All couples have problems. I can forgive the occasional fight.

You have whisked away with the person that you believe that you will spend forever with. The relationship has moved so quickly. You assume that this is because they are so passionate. You are accountable for their every word; you would have done anything to please them, and you tried. More and more, they became frustrated with you. They forcefully criticize the way that you speak, dress, look, and behave. No matter how much you workshop your actions, you never seem to get it quite right. It felt like your fault.

You had only ever wanted to be loved and to love them. You were bewildered and blindsided by their hatred. It has burned away a part of your soul. They still claim to love you, but they seem to enjoy crushing you beneath their weighted thumb as though you were some errant insect.

When they bonded to you initially, it was more than the word “bond” can express. It felt as though they welded your heart to their own. Their passing moments of kindness leave you with a thought that destroys you: what if there is hope? What if this is still the person that I love? You eventually found yourself doing everything in your power to dwell in those moments. You were walking on eggshells around the person that you loved, to keep them from ripping you apart again.

You understood that something wasn't right, but you would never have guessed that everything was fake.

Eventually, you are forced to consider that maybe they never loved you. Maybe it was all an act. Those gentle transient moments of happiness worked against you still, but your brain was telling you that they were destroying you for sport. Your partner seemed to derive pleasure from hurting others. They enjoyed starting fights in public and wearing people down. The mask began to fall away.

Know that you are not alone. The reason that you were pulled into this trap, to begin with, is because you are empathetic. It doesn't matter your gender or your race; you are not weak for this. You are caring. You saw someone willing to eat up the love that you had been dying to give. It looked like a perfect opportunity. So many people fall into this same trap. Held fast by the heart that is being worn down by their abuser.

There is a moment of abject terror when you first realize that you are not going to stay, that none of this is sustainable. It is the realization that you will have to make one of the hardest decisions you have ever had to make. You are going to have to fight. You have known this person for so long. You know from that experience that leaving isn't going to be easy. That they aren't just going to allow you to

Leaving is the bravest thing that you will ever do. There is so much talk of logic and understanding. None of these things matter at the moment. You can prepare for the moment for years, but it will take every ounce of courage you have within yourself. It is going to be so hard, but so worth it. The moment that you utter those words, you are taking back your love from someone who used it against you. You are giving it back to yourself.

Prepare for the Backlash

Different partners will react in different ways to the news that they are being broken up with. Codependent partners will use guilt and emotional blackmail as a weapon to win your affections back. Be prepared for threats of harm to themselves and being told that you are leaving them when they need you the most. Remember that you are not responsible for the emotional welfare of anyone other than yourself.

Stay Firm

Your partner will do everything they can to bring you back to the relationship, kicking and screaming.

When it looks like they have moved on, they will still be looking for ways to suck you back in. They will use others to prove their worth to you so that you fold and accept them back.

You coming back to the relationship can be seen as an incentive. Abusers are capable of changing their behavior when it is incentivized. They will make promises to you that they will treat you differently. This person is going to agree to be the person that you have always needed them to be. Do NOT fall for this. Their changes will last only as long as the incentive lasts. The moment that you accept the abusive partner back, they will begin to fall back into old habits. Their behavior change will not only change, but they will also hold your attempt to leave over your head. They will label your dash for freedom as a betrayal.

From the moment you decide that you will walk away, allow yourself to come to terms with the idea that your story will be told. When you feel weak, talk to a parent or a friend. Tell them the truth. This is going to allow you a chance to see the situation through someone else's eyes, someone who loves you. They are going to be horrified. They are going to offer to help you. Hold on to the sadness that they feel for the way that you have been treated. Use their outrage as gasoline when your resolve begins to sputter.

The Plan

The nature of these relationships makes it necessary to limit contact after ties have been cut. These partners will use any excuse to lure you back in with promises of change. There will be offers of vacations, vehicles, or material objects that you have expressed interest in.

Do your best to develop a plan of action. Secure employment or a place to live upon leaving these partners, if possible. If this isn't possible, then contact a family or advocacy group that will be willing to assist you with these goals when you have fled.

Abusive partners can be potentially dangerous and may threaten you with violence or self-harm. The breakup needs to happen swiftly and with someone waiting in the wings to serve as a getaway driver.

Emotionally Brace Yourself

You will never be sure of your decision to leave. There will always be this sinking feeling that you are not making the right decision.

That you will not be able to make it on your own, or that your partner will not be able to live without you. These are the feelings that you need to make peace with. Confusing emotions plague breakups of any variety.

Allow yourself to live in what your future will be like. Once you have freed yourself from an unhealthy relationship, you have the potential to do anything you wish to. Be anyone you want to be. You only have to make it through this rough patch, and the pain that you have learned to live with will finally begin to dissipate. Your freedom is worth the hardship that you will endure.

love.

CHAPTER 7 - Dominate Yourself in Love

In a normal relationship, it is natural for the individuals involved to depend on one another. However, a codependent relationship is different. It is not like the dependency you see in a healthy relationship.

What Does a Healthy Relationship Look Like?

We are social beings and have lived in groups relying on our survival, food, and shelter. It is therefore not wrong to need others and rely on them when you need help. This type of healthy dependency is termed interdependency.

The normal dependent relationship is a healthy one where there is a mutual sharing of support, help, and encouragement.

But in a codependent relationship, there is a gross imbalance. One person keeps sacrificing for the other without receiving anything in return.

This is a toxic relationship that results in burnout, dissatisfaction, and resentment.

There is enhanced self-esteem, mutual respect, confidence, master, and emotional security in a healthy interdependent relationship.

The help, support, and encouragement you get from your partner will help you feel safe and confident in tackling any issues you face. It will allow you to overcome any fear and help you grow as an individual.

Thus, there is a perfect balance of independence and dependence. Healthy interdependence does not prevent you from forging ahead and provides you with the prop you need to improve yourself.

In an interdependent relationship, the persons involved will feel competent and express their needs. They accept help from others but do not depend on them to improve their self-esteem.

In a codependent relationship, the codependent person is not aware of who they are, what they want, and how to live as a separate identity.

In short, in a normal and healthy interdependent relationship, your identity is not compromised. You can receive and give help while retaining your autonomy and individuality.

Why Is Codependency Unhealthy?

In a codependent relationship, there is over-dependence of one person on another. You feel your identity is fully intermeshed with that of your partner.

Your focus is to such a magnitude that your goals, interests, and needs are ignored or suppressed.

While you may hold a job and are capable of paying bills and taking care of your children, you have this unhealthy desire to feel needed. This desire makes you dependent so you can stay feeling lovable and worthy.

Self-worth for a codependent is based on fixing, helping, and rescuing others. This causes an imbalance in the relationship.

Only when both individuals involved accept their roles of giver and taker can the codependent relationship work.

However, it is not at all healthy to sacrifice your needs to feel valued and accepted. This is because the unworthy and flawed feeling creates toxic dependency where you always look to others to validate your beliefs, interests, and existence.

The need or craving to be wanted can leave you trapped in an unhappy, unfulfilling, and abusive relationship. Without the caregiver role, you will feel unloved and purposeless.

Enabling is different from helping

There is mutual support and help in a healthy interdependent relationship where each person has room to grow.

On the other hand, a codependent relationship has one person as an enabler, doing or rescuing things for the other instead of helping the partner to do things on their own.

The craving for being needed is compelling, and it unconsciously makes you an enabler. The enabled partner will be dependent and dysfunctional as if they are healthy, sober, or employed, and you will lose your purpose of taking care of them. Without the purpose, you will feel unworthy.

This triggers you into acting so that you persistently nag and give unnecessary advice. Helping and enabling differ as helping encourages you to become confident and self-sufficient.

Codependency affects growth

Unlike an interdependent relationship where the people involved are encouraged to grow in all aspects, including professional, emotional, spiritual, and social, a codependent relationship is abusive and unhealthy.

This is because the relationship concentrates on maintaining an imbalance where the giver can go on giving and gain self-esteem by enabling. At the same time, the taker has his financial, emotional, and physical needs met.

Codependent persons will find it very difficult to function independently due to their self-worth issues and their constant need to rely on others.

While a relationship is vital to your existence, adding joy and satisfaction to your life cannot fix the underlying wounds you carry into a relationship.

You replay the dysfunctional relationship dynamics and worsen the relationship until the root cause is healed.

Understanding codependency and interdependency

It is difficult to recognize the difference between interdependent and codependent relationships if you have never been exposed to a normal and healthy relationship.

Here is a table from Webster University on differences between the two relationships. The table will help you clear any doubts you have regarding the nature of your relationship or how a normal and healthy one can look like.

Although the two relationships' differences are apparent, you may still not recognize you are in a codependent relationship that easily.

You have to put in real effort to reflect on your situation and be honest with your feelings. Even if you become aware of the relationship, refraining from such behavior is difficult. It needs perseverance and a strong will to break the chain and get help to heal and resume a normal and healthy relationship.

CHAPTER 8 - Examples of Codependency in Relationships

Workaholism

It is not necessarily wrong to be a workaholic; the motivation is right. However, if one overworks themselves, thinking that by doing so much, they will earn the approval, praise, and respect of their partner, that is not the right motivation. While you may earn the desired approval you need, it will not take long before you notice its effects on your health. You likely have a lazy partner who does not want to play their duty, and that should not cost your well-being at what you do. There is no heroism in overworking.

Taking the Blame

Your spouse, out of their careless behavior, loses a promising contract. When they inform you, you do not only feel sorry for them, you also claim your responsibility in it, thinking you did not support them in a way or two, which you know would not be necessary anyway, or are farfetched. You want to take responsibility so that your spouse is relieved of their horrible feeling. When they feel low, you fear that they will withdraw their love, attention, and affection from you. You want to prevent that, so you sacrifice your feelings for theirs. Then they see that you could probably have done better, not them, and that is where you go wrong. They stop looking inwards and instead shift their blame on you for what you are not responsible for. Over time, you begin to become aggressive, as it begins to overwhelm you. Your spouse will never do anything wrong with themselves, but everything is wrong with you and will not improve.

Undue Anxiety

Your partner hits their leg on the wall, and you feel the pain. They do not get to bed in time or experience shallow sleep, and you begin to have sleepless nights. Their problems concern you more than them. You wear away while they watch helplessly. You want to show them you care, yes, but you are overreacting due to your insecurities. Your partner may esteem you for it, but that will not heal you. Everyone has their worries, and only relevant support is needed to be back at what they do to address their issues.

Manipulation

The kind here is twisting your partner's ill or evil responses to comfort yourself. Your partner called you 'stupid,' and you think they did not mean it. They were joking or playing with you, you think. By the time you realize what is going on, you have been on the receiving end of verbal abuse getting worse and worse each time, and you have never tried to do anything to stop it. You keep agreeing to such abuses because you do not want to be abandoned. On their end, your spouse keeps throwing their abuses because they know you can only take it anyway. You accept to be nothing so that they can be everything hoping you will keep the peace that way forever. Healthy relationships require partners to regard each other with respect both on the inside and on the outside.

Feeling Unlovable

Do you feel the love of your partner yourself, or do you just think and hope they love you? By the time this question begins to take a few of your thoughts, you can be sure that their commitment to you and the relationship decreases. When it exists between the two of you, love is not suspected, though, or imagined. It is experienced then felt. Living in speculation of your partner's love for you is a consequence of a codependent who has less regard for themselves – abdicating their worth, esteem, and dignity to promote that of their partner.

Change Your Partner

Healthy relationships are those in which partners accept each other as they are. They know the beauty of their differences. The codependent tries to change their partner. You think they will become better lovable to you when they change their identity to a certain degree. You want to improve on their version to some degree. You are trying to protect them against themselves by removing them from their current state. You think they will harm themselves in their current state. This fear is typically exaggerated, leading to breaking your friendship with you in the first place. No one changes unless they find a need and accept it by themselves.

Unnecessary Cover-Ups

Your spouse does something wrong, and you sweep it under the carpet so that they may not suffer the consequences of their actions. Over time, they live expecting that they can do all manner of things and find cover in you. If not addressed and overcome in time, a promiscuous behavior such as lying to your partner will get back at and overcome you as well. Falsehood can only be hidden for a while. With time, when discovered, you will be ridiculed and judged for covering up for your partner. Initially, you thought you were doing it in good faith.

Neglecting Yourself and Your Needs

True, sometimes you deny yourself for the sake of your partner. Codependents skip their pressing need to attend to their partner's usual wants. What is more, the recipient is either not willing or indifferent. However, you force yourself on them because you consider them more important than yourself, therefore seeking their approval of you. There is no point in that. You are the performer, but you seek the approval of a non-performer over what they do not even understand.

Intruding

Your partner is always on you, following where you go, how you spend, picking your belongings and using them, and not allowing you space to breathe your air. You look at trespass in the face and then yield to your low self-esteem and keep quiet or appear welcome altogether. This is a behavioral defect that will soon make you lose not just your head but your whole self.

Excessive Obligation

You are always looking out to fulfill your partner's needs without considering your own. You speed up or slow down to your partner's pace, and your sense is not comfortable with you, but stick at it. In a healthy relationship, every partner helps the other be their best selves and supplement and reciprocate their efforts to not hampered individual progress. We dare put it to you that codependents put excessive obligations on themselves without their partners' prior request.

CHAPTER 9 - Important Codependency Relapse Tips

Are you among those people who are unaware of or very scared about codependency relapse? If yes, then you are in the right place at present. A codependent individual can recover by pursuing proper treatment and therapies. But the signs or symptoms of codependency may return even after treatment. But you need not worry at all. First of all, every single family member and closed or loved ones of a recovered codependent person need to realize that relapse of the past signs may occur, but that does not mean failure. Many experts often state that relapse is the signal that the interference of new treatment is necessary.

The reasons or triggers of relapse are not the same for all codependent people, and the reasons keep on varying. For example, maybe the basic or primary treatment facility or procedure is not up to the mark. Or maybe the person suffering from co-dependency did not commit or respond adequately to the recovery procedure. Stress, discontinuing aftercare such as stopping therapy, not getting adequate positive motivation from family members or life partner, etc., are other causes of co-dependency relapse. The signs of relapse can be observed after a few weeks, months, or years. Moreover, not all codependent individuals who have once gone through the treatment need to show relapse signs. Family members or well-wishers must not lose hope and continue supporting the person who is suffering due to codependency relapse and encourage them and help to see dreams of a brighter and better future. You will undoubtedly be thrilled to learn or know that relapse can be dealt with or prevented. You may come across many ways with the help of which relapse of codependency can be well prevented. Here you will get to know about some of the critical tips or ways for ceasing codependency relapse.

Identify the Signs

Are you getting excessively involved with some issues of other people? Or are you again trying to please others and waiting for their approval? Are you again facing a problem in making your decisions? Are you getting the same feeling once again that you are unworthy or unimportant to your friends, family, and colleagues? It is no doubt that all the facts mentioned earlier are the signs of codependency relapse. But that does not mean you have to start worrying about it. Maybe you are experiencing the codependency patterns once again, but you will certainly get rid of them by giving it another effective try. The first and foremost way of preventing relapse is by recognizing or observing the relapse signs. A person who has overcome codependency, including his or her family members, life partners, or friends, must stay aware of the return of the undesired symptoms. Once an individual can do the following step, it becomes relatively easy to proceed towards the further steps of codependency relapse prevention.

Stay in Touch with Mentors

Another effective way of dealing with codependency relapse is by having connections with your mentors. He or she will be able to assist you in leading a positive and healthy life. It does not mean that you need to contact or talk with your mentor only when you observe any signs of codependency relapse. A connection with them may prove fruitful even when no signs of relapse exist after recovering from codependency or a codependent relationship. Many individuals are present who believe that a mentor has to be a professional person. But it is not mandatory that a mentor has to be professional by nature. He or she can be your friend, colleague, well-wisher, etc. The only compulsory part is that a mentor must be a person who possesses excellent judgment and is also very much sensible. A person with such characteristics will surely help you by letting you choose the right track and motivate you in all possible situations. If it is necessary, then you may need to reset all your boundaries regarding your work schedule. Staying in touch does not mean that you must have face to face or phone conversation all the time. If you find it quite disturbing, then you need not answer calls. Contact can be kept through text messages and e-mail, and such ways of transmitting messages are helpful.

Try Different or New Methods for Solving Problems

Often, a codependent person faces difficulty in solving problems by himself or herself. Making firm decisions and moving forward either by ignoring or solving any sort of problem is not at all easy for people with codependency. Such signs may come back even after recovering from codependency. As soon as the relapse occurs, that same person may again feel helpless and find themselves stuck in between problems. Thus, it is necessary to plan new or updated tactics for solving problems. It is also necessary to possess different coping skills because a limited number of skills may not prove beneficial in all issues. You need to make up a healthy mindset that if a method of handling a problem fails, you need not feel depressed or unworthy and immediately try another method. Read journals that are based on positive and motivational thoughts, ways of being confident, etc. By reading such journals, you may gain back your lost self-confidence, feel your worth, get new ideas for dealing with problems, and create a positive mindset.

Follow Aftercare or Post-Treatment Plan

In this matter, family members, including parents, siblings, life partners, etc., have to be very aware. There is no such certainty that a person who has overcome co-dependency will never show any signs of relapse or co-dependency has been eliminated from his or her life. Thus, family members and well-wishers have to stay healthy and follow all the required aftercare treatment procedures as much as possible. Close relatives or well-wishers need to encourage or motivate the codependent individual's family members to maintain their roles properly. Even they need encouragement as such people are not at all addiction professionals. Whenever someone who overcame codependency faces signs of relapse, their family members need to stay beside and give proper guidance by referring them back to an effective treatment plan. At times, the individual facing relapse of codependent behaviors may not be willing to go through any treatment procedure once again. Even if they do not want to do so, constant motivation is required for seeking professional support from counselors, therapists, proficient recovery groups, etc.

Find Out Ways for Stopping Obsession

Many recovered codependent individuals face the problem of obsession. If you also face the same problem, you need to find various effective ways of stopping it. A lot of people begin to quiet his or her mind to recover from this state. You may practice meditation regularly. It will work wonders for calming down your mind. Another useful tool for dealing with this problem is hiking. You may take long walks to any bright, cold, or pleasant place of your choice, and walking is considered one of the best exercises. Thus, hiking is treated as a magical and scientific way of calming down your brain. Does any sort of activities of your choice that will calm your brain? You may write down your assignments or projects, practice spiritual reading, etc.

Control Your Feelings

Feelings do exist in almost every single individual on the planet earth. Feelings vary from one person to the other. Having frustrating feelings or feeling sad as well as happy is quite familiar. If you have recovered from codependency, it does not mean that you don't have the right to express your feelings or feel sad. Everyone has the right to express their natural feelings. That does not mean you have to feel frustrated and sad if you cannot control something or someone. A lot of recovered codependent individuals exhibit this relapse sign. It is not the same as directly controlling the other person. If you or any of your closed ones show such a sign even after going through proper and professional treatment, it is a matter of trouble. Thus, it is better to start controlling your feelings or seek professional guidance for better assistance.

Focus on Today

To get a new and healthy lifestyle and kicking off codependency relapse, you need to stop thinking about your memories and bad experiences. Your focus should only be on today. Being mindful and thinking of ways to make the present-day fruitful should be your aim. Stop worrying about tomorrow.

CHAPTER 10 - Boosting Your Self Esteem

One proper antidote to manipulative behavior, in general, incorporates jealousy; it is in raising one's self-esteem and self-worth. It's the one overriding factor that protects you from just about all negative emotions that arise in you and those emanating from others.

It is not some clever tactic or trick to deflect negative comments or anything like that, but instead, raising your self-confidence aids in diffusing the impact jealous actions wear you from the get-go. It inoculates you from ever suffering from malicious behavior in the first place, as these kinds of feelings are typically unconscious acts played out by those experiencing low confidence or temporary vulnerability.

Nobody will genuinely feel jealous if they have high regard for themselves. In truth, nothing is more important than how you think and feel about yourself; that goes for relationships also as life in general.

Handle Your Inner Critic

You have an inner critic; everyone does. Taking note of this voice can help get things done or help you do the things that will gain acceptance from people. But this inner critic also can kill your self-esteem if you let it. Suppose you permit this egoic element of your personality to get out of hand.

Over-thinking situations are not a good thing to do; I might go as far as to say it's the essential plight of human civilization today.

It is usual for your inner voice to suggest both positive and negative thoughts. It is not about blocking out the noise. But instead, analyzing what you are thinking and if it is of any benefit to you? If it is not, then it is important to stop yourself from going into the rabbit hole of negative and spiraling imaginary scenarios.

Refocus those negative thoughts into something constructive and happier.

Cultivate a Gratitude Mindset

I used to think that being grateful for the sake of it was silly. Why would I appreciate everything I had in my life now? My goals were much more extensive and loftier. Wouldn't this be me thinking small and making do? Not! The mind works in a way to serve you more of what you are currently experiencing now. If you are frequently in a state of fear and worry, guess what. Your subconscious will simply serve you up more to be fearful and worried about.

On the other hand, if you are incredibly flattering and grateful in the here and now, the mind goes to work to find you more of the same! The subconscious does not know the difference between feeling great because you won the lottery and being ecstatic to be alive. It works in feelings, emotions, and imagery.

In this regard, learning to understand yourself and every one of the great things about your life, including your current relationship, is a great exercise to do. As a bonus to this, when you feel good about yourself and grateful for the things that you do have, large or small, your mind won't have room to entertain negative thoughts.

Most of the suffering people undergo in their lives is imaginary anyway. It is created from the dissonance between where they are and where they think they might wish to be. But that is a false horizon; if you cannot be proud of the journey, you can never be content with wherever you are heading, as there will always be the following thing when you get there.

Again, the trick is to be happy now. I do know this sounds oversimplified and easier said than done, but it is the one thing that gave me the most joy in life when I was battling with my business in the early days.

It has been shown that the top business professionals in the world do that (and all successful people in general). If they are currently at point 'B' in their lives, they do not look forward to pointing 'C' and say, "look how far I even have to travel." Whenever you are trying to chase after it, it disappears further into space.

Instead, what these people do is reminisce at point 'A' to where they started and say, "Hey, look how far I have come!" this is often a subtle change of outlook, but I promise you, if you do make this one adjustment in your thinking your whole outlook on life will change, and for the better. You will instantly start feeling grateful and satisfied with your current lot and far less frustrated with not yet being where you think that you ought to be. Remember that the subconscious aims to serve you more of what you are feeling at the moment. If you are abundantly happy and grateful for what is in your present existence, it will find other such situations to bring your way.

My past business partner used to valet his car outside of his favorite restaurant in the city each week. However, he could never understand why the parking attendant would always place his car two blocks away, rather than just across the road as he'd instructed. He would get so frustrated by having to walk an additional 5 minutes for his vehicle each time; it almost sent him into a frenzy. He would ask me what he should do about it, as he noticed I used to be much calmer in similar situations.

I simply asked him to think about it for a moment. What would he rather be, a well-paid businessman who had the chance to valet his top of the range BMW at his favorite restaurant each week? But need to wait an additional 5 minutes for it each time he left. Or be the guy who has got to valet cars and survive off tips for a living? His outlook on things immediately changed. "You are right, he replied; what was I thinking? I'll give the guy an opportunity from now on".

Put Things into Writing

You can also write down what you like about yourself in a journal, the positive traits you have, and the situations they affect. When you are feeling low, or when the day is not going as you'd hoped, or when negative thoughts begin to creep into your mind, remove your journal and re-read them. You can update this list daily or whenever you discover something new and positive about yourself.

It is good to start your day by going over these statements as they work a bit like affirmations. You cultivate the positive emotions surrounding these attributes or events and allow you to feel them again in the here and now. Remember, the brain has no way of telling the difference regarding emotions, i.e., the event might be happening now, ten years ago, or how into the future!

Stop Being a Perfectionist

Aiming for perfection all of the time is often very destructive. A bit like negative thoughts, perfectionism can paralyze you from getting things done due to your fear of not living up to a high standard you have set for yourself. This behavior might also end in procrastination, thus ending up not getting you the expected results. This way may bring your self-esteem crashing down if you let it.

Try making these alterations in your thinking to overcome perfectionism:

Strive for good enough. Stop aiming for perfection; remember, nobody's perfect. When you aim for perfection all of the time, you won't finish any task because you might either wait for the proper time or still work on the job until it seems flawless (which will never happen).

Striving for perfection will only hurt you at the end of the day. Remind yourself that life isn't a fairy tale that always ends with a happily ever after. Learn to manage your expectations, because in most cases, this is often the reality. You have managed to deal with everything life has thrown at you until now. How do I know this? Because you are still alive reading this today. The real curveballs in life you can never see coming, so there is absolutely no point in worrying about them today. You can deal with them at the time as you usually have done, so stop worrying.

Look at Mistakes and Failure as Lessons

Let us just say that it is inevitable you will make mistakes from time to time. You may fail on some days. But the great thing about experiencing failures and committing errors is that there are lessons to be gleaned from all of them.

There will always be positives you can take from every situation; you only need to determine what they are. Learn from them and internalize this stuff and come back stronger. "You either win or you learn," as they say; I couldn't agree more.

Similar to this, you usually got to try something new. Get out of your comfort zone as much and as often as possible. This way is often the only proper route to feeling content and successful in life. Having new experiences and learning new things that will feed into your positive confidence and self-esteem feedback loops.

They do not have to be big and scary all of the time, and just small wins; incremental progress will do the work. As long as you are moving in the right direction, that is all that counts.

Stop Comparing Yourself to Others

You will never be good enough if you keep on comparing yourself with other people. You can never win because there is always someone better, or there is still something more valuable to achieve out there. You are only ever in a competition with yourself to enhance your version from yesterday or a year ago.

Remember to always reminisce at 'A,' not looking forward to 'C.' Look at how far you have come as an individual regarding your development. People are on their journey; allow them to get on with it. Only you walk in your shoes, be pleased with that, and keep treading your path.

Be Around People That Are Supportive of You

This way is fairly obvious, but most people still don't take so much notice of this idea as they ought to. It is simple; don't hang around negative people who only see what you have done wrong. This way includes jealous people!

It is said that you are the mixture of the five people you most ordinarily associate with. Or show me your friends and I will show you your future kind of deal. This way often is because we adjust our behavior in line with these people accordingly. That goes for everything from mannerisms, speaking styles to the quantity of cash most are making. You can adjust your thermostat in all categories to meet the mean of this peer group.

So, try to be around positive and high-performance people, those that are willing to support you and lift you. This way is often easier said than done regarding shutting friends and family, but you need to draw the line somewhere. Be with people that will pick you up when you fall and help you stand on your feet again.

CHAPTER 11 - A Guide to Recovery through Mindfulness

We have exposed codependency for what it is, where it comes from, and how it sabotages our lives. Hopefully, you have been working on remembering and writing. This was hard because it took time, focus, and honesty (and the first two are always in short supply for us). It may have triggered uncomfortable emotions. Every time I sat down to work on this project, my heart would race. Feelings remain. Changing the way I respond to those feelings is what has turned my life around.

Now the arduous work begins: making the changes that will help you reclaim your life. The reason this part is so difficult is that it requires four commitments people like us can't easily make:

1. Setting aside time to concentrate on your well-being. Codependents are historically not very good at doing this. You will be fighting your own, non-stop, reasoning mind, which will tell you there isn't time, you don't have the energy, and you already know what to do.

2. Being willing to see yourself from a new perspective. This will also be hard because you've spent your entire life with a distorted concept of who you are.

3. You have got to be ready to go from knowing in your head to do. This may be the hardest of all because all those

automatic behaviors - while not leading to the positive outcomes you hoped for - are natural to you. Nevertheless, you will have to do things that go completely against your nature, such as not striving for perfection. There is no one right way or answer. It's all unique to you. You can't let your feelings of guilt run your actions because you think you're not doing it correctly enough. Everything that is codependency is going to be working against you here.

4. Most importantly, you have to believe you can be transformed into the healthy being you want to become. You must see yourself with a fresh and balanced mind, an energetic body, and a lifestyle.

Do you want this or not? Are you willing to stop making excuses, get past self-pity, guilt, and the ever-present hopelessness you live with, and do the real work of healing?

If you are genuinely ready to change your life for the better, then this Guide will be a vital tool for you. It's not magic. It's a makeover of your thinking, your words, your actions, and your surroundings. Nothing is going to take you from miserable to happy overnight. But you are going to learn to use some new muscles–Maybe for a few months, perhaps for life. It's good any way you want and needs to do it.

Let's agree it's going to be hard but certainly not impossible. You have figured out –I hope– by now that it's futile trying to change or fix others. So, you might as well put your energy to fair use and do what you can to change yourself. Everything I will be laying out for you is entirely within your reach. I'm not asking you to try anything I haven't done. As with anything in life, you will want to take from all of this what works for you. Some of it won't be a good fit. That's okay. Flexibility is an uncomfortable concept because, in our thinking, rigidity rules. Things make sense that way. Be willing to get past this urge and step into the realm of possibilities.

Have you ever tried telling someone information that would help their situation only to have them chant over and over again, "I know, I know?" But nothing changes because it's just head knowledge. They haven't done the work of actually changing. Codependent people are great at that. Remember this as you read and say to yourself, "I already know that." Knowing and doing are different. Decide to let yourself be immersed in new ideas and practices, which may at first seem far-fetched or something you've tried before in a half-hearted manner. Do them without judging or rationalizing. If you try and can't do that, walk away and come back when you're ready to try again. It will all be there when you're less anxious.

I need to stress to you again that what I offer are exercises that helped me. The information in the Guide is a compilation of information, beliefs, and actions which, over the years, proved to be life-altering to many people, including me.

CHAPTER 12 - Being Assertive

Perhaps at this point, you are beginning to realize what a big challenge you are facing as you work to put your codependence behind you. You know you need to take charge of your boundaries, but you just don't have the tools you need to do it. It can seem very scary, but you can keep going through your fear. The first step to reclaiming your boundaries is to learn to be assertive.

What Is Being Assertive?

Being assertive means standing up for yourself robustly and confidently. When you are assertive, you respect your position as well as the positions of others. You tell people clearly and honestly how you feel, what you think, and what you need.

Assertiveness is very uncommon on both sides of a codependent relationship. The three other types of communication are passive, aggressive, and passive-aggressive. As a partner in a codependent relationship, you likely relied on these other forms of communication to try and get what you wanted.

You communicate passively when you let everything happen as it will. You give little or no input into the conversation. When you do say something, you let others convince you that you are wrong. Your partner dominates the relationship, and you are merely along for the ride. People who choose to communicate passively usually fear rejection or confrontations.

When you communicate aggressively, you push the other person into doing what you want. You are usually hostile and angry, or you complain loudly and nag your partner to quit his addictive behavior. You insist on having your way, no matter how the other person feels. You use punishments, demands, and blaming to assert your dominance. If you are an aggressive communicator, you do not concern yourself with your partner's rights and opinions.

Often, people who are in a codependent relationship become passive-aggressive. They have their feelings and opinions about family situations.

But they do not express themselves honestly and openly. Instead, they manipulate or trick their partner into doing things the way they want them done.

When you choose to be assertive, you decrease misunderstandings. Your partner knows what you want, whether he acts to give it to you or not. You do not try to control your partner. You do take away your partner's power over your life.

o How to Be Assertive?

Being assertive with your partner for the first time is a big hurdle to cross. Once you have established that you will only participate in healthy communications, you change the relationship drastically. And, if you want to stop being codependent, that is precisely what you need to do. Here is a step-by-step guide to help you through those first assertive communications.

Step One: Decide What You Want to Communicate

Deciding what to talk about is not as easy as it sounds. If you are in a codependent relationship, you are more accustomed to talking about your partner and what they need to do. Instead, focus on your wants, needs, feelings, and opinions. Start by talking about just one thing you want to say about yourself.

Step Two: Speak Clearly and Honestly

When you are in a codependent relationship with an addict, it is easy to think first about saying things in a way your partner will accept. Or, conversely, you might be prone to pushing his buttons and provoking him to lash out at you. This time, just think about expressing your thought or feeling in a way your partner will understand. To speak assertively, you have to be honest and give your partner the message in your heart.

Step Three: Let Your Partner Own His Feelings and Responses

Right now, you might be thinking about how your partner might react if you speak clearly and honestly about your thoughts and feelings. And the truth is that he might get very upset or withdrawn. He might become angry with you and become verbally abusive. You need to know that before you start being assertive.

Just remember that whatever your partner says, does, or seems to think or feel, is something that belongs to him and him alone. You do not have to feel bad for stating your opinion. You do not have to take abuse for expressing your feelings. You have every right to speak assertively.

Step Four: Respect Your Partner's Rights

One of the hallmarks of healthy and assertive communications is maintaining respect for the other person's rights. An addict can become so wrapped up in his addiction that he allows other people to make his decisions and tell him what is right or wrong for him. You might even feel justified in disrespecting his boundaries because he is in no shape to know what he wants.

But you can still practice being assertive regardless of your partner's addiction. Speak up and say what you want or need to say. At the same time, give him the consideration of respecting his thoughts, feelings, and opinions.

Learning to be assertive is, for most people, a lifetime task. You can begin with just a few assertive conversations a day and increase them as you get the hang of it. Eventually, you learn to communicate assertively in every conversation.

While there will always be the temptation to resort to being passive, passive-aggressive, or aggressive, you have the power to choose assertiveness.

Your life will not always be more comfortable, but it will be healthier. You develop a better sense of self-esteem as you speak and act assertively. The reverse is also true: when you feel better about yourself, it is easier to stand up for your own needs and wants. And now we come to the heart of the codependent relationship. You need to improve your self-esteem if you want to break free of codependency and move on with your life.

CHAPTER 13 - Being in a Relationship with Someone with Codependency

People have relationship crises because their expectations for a relationship are generally unrealistic. As we've said before, the partners' connections are almost always made at the sub-conscious level. Such a crisis is defined as a brief psychic disturbance that, from time to time, occurs in people struggling with life problems that exceed their capacity to cope. The crisis appears as a functional disorder in the mental, emotional, and behavioral plane. It manifests through ego dysfunction, intellectual inefficiency, disrupted concentration, and reasoning on the mental plane. In contrast, there is a fear of abandonment on the emotional plane, sleep disorders, altered sex drives, and eating disorders.

There are often problems in the relationship that partners can resolve without an expert's help, but problems require the expert or psychotherapist's help. Even couples who have successfully overcome serious problems may critically encounter codependency problems when examining their partner's choice in their relationship. In assessing one's emotional life, a person will compare past expectations with what is happening in the present. If expectations are not met, there is a problem with the relationship.

- ### How to Solve a Relationship Crisis Caused by Codependency?

Daily communication between partners plays a vital role in the partnership. It is essential for the couple that both parties be able to speak and express emotions. All couples should make an effort to understand and respect one another and to nurture common values. It is necessary to develop empathy, respect, and tolerance. Partners need to define the problems in the relationship and offer solutions. Placing the blame on one another is a significant problem relationship and leads to additional conflict. Avoiding problems and postponing communications also deepen the conflict. So, one should talk about the problem, not run away from it. The cornerstone of a quality partnership is the belief that their partner is worthy of respect and appreciation.

- ### Does Affective Attachment Style Affect the Quality of The Partnership?

Philosophers, psychologists, and writers have all tried their hand at addressing the question of what people want in a partnership. Nietzsche claimed that a man wants two things —danger and play. Freud concluded that women do not know what they want, but these explanations do not answer the question. There should be moments in each person's life to contemplate what they want in a partner and the ideal emotional connection level. A partnership's qualities depend on many factors, such as intimate interactions, loyalty, communication, relationship satisfaction, sexual satisfaction, support, etc. An emotional partner is the primary provider and recipient of emotional support, a sexual partner, and an influential figure. Depending on the affective pattern formed, the partners will exhibit a degree of care and sexuality.

Affective attachment is manifested differently in codependent people, so in a partner relationship, individual differences are determined by useful attachment patterns. Kim Bartolomeu talked about four styles of attachment, 1) safe, 2) preoccupied, 3) timid, and 4) dismissive. Safe individuals build open and authentic partnerships, have high self-confidence, quickly achieve intimacy in relationships, and constructively resolve conflicts. For people with this pattern of affective attachment, emotional intercourse with others is very important. In the partnership, they are securely attached because they enjoy the closeness and intimacy and feel self-worth.

On the other hand, codependent persons are dependent on partners, invest too much in a partnership, and believe that they must be loved. These persons are territorial in representing their love and idealizing their partner. Afflicted persons have a conflict of motives and seek affirmation of their partners' values, and they are passive and dependent. Chaos is the prominent feature of their relationships. They avoid bonding with compulsively self-reliant people, superior, and have an increased need for autonomy. They build short-term and superficial connections. Lack of closeness, intimacy, and expression of emotions are their characteristics. They have the conviction that the relationship suffocates, but the root of the fear is rejection. Various worldwide studies show that securely bonded couples work better together, are more satisfied in the relationship, and constructively resolve conflicts. According to behavioral theory, compatible partner behaviors lead to higher quality partnerships.

o Same or Different Styles of Attachment

Research shows that dyads in which both members have a secure attachment style are of better quality. The same behavioral system and emotional response, the experience of acceptance, support, availability, and sensitivity of the partners lead to these couples having a good relationship. Couples in which the dyad members are differently related are likely to rate their relationship as lower quality due to differences in the behavioral, cognitive, and emotional systems. One member who suffers from codependency may have a high level of anxiety accompanied by fear of abandonment. In contrast, the other may have a low level of anxiety accompanied by an experience of self-worth. The same rule applies to the avoidance domain. One partner may express and accept trust and closeness; the other may be distrustful and disinterested in expressing closeness. These differences lead to frequent marital conflicts, dissatisfaction, misunderstandings, and inconsistencies, affecting marriage quality. Married couples who share the same anxiety and avoidance levels will have a higher quality relationship than couples with disparate anxiety and avoidance levels.

- ### Relationship with a Codependent Person

You have been in an emotional relationship for a long time, and everything seems to be okay. Your partner is fully committed, and you feel loved. However, that doesn't make you happy. You have the feeling that you have lost yourself. You cannot distinguish your wants from your partner's needs. You are chronically dissatisfied, even depressed. You feel like you are in a cage and as though you are no longer you. These signals can indicate that you are in a symbiotic emotional relationship.

- ### What Is a Symbiotic Emotional Relationship?

The term symbiotic relationship is commonly used to describe the type of relationship in an animal species. It is a relationship in which two individuals interact with each other for their common benefit. These individuals are functionally and physically connected and operate as one organism. In humans, the symbiotic relationship is the fusion of two people into one, meaning they cannot function effectively without each other. Practically speaking, you and I become we, a new plane of existence in which both persons lose their individuality. This kind of relationship is not exclusive to partners in a relationship or marriage. It may also be present in relationships with friends or parent-child relationships.

○ What Kinds of Persons Are Inclined to Build Symbiotic Relationships?

Although relationships between partners imply equality, one person can be drawn into a symbiotic relationship by the other. Usually, this happens under the guise of true love. That is to say, one of the partners involved is very happy because they have received unconditional love and commitment from the other partner. It is essential to understand that a symbiotic relationship is entirely normal in the early stage of a relationship and can last for several months.

The partners are in a state of falling in love, so they feel like one being.

They are oblivious to those around them. Still, this is just a phase and should by no means persist long-term.

People who build purely symbiotic emotional relationships have a fear of being left behind/rejected. Usually, such persons have had harrowing experiences in their lives. Experiences in primary family relationships or past partnerships (because of the condition they suffer) want to avoid repeating at all costs. To ensure that such experiences are not repeated, they fully commit to their partner and demand that they do so in return.

The person also tries to compensate for emotional losses that occurred in past relationships by intensifying the current one, which results in a pang of hunger for constant attention and closeness.

These are generally addictive personality types that cannot function independently and seek a robust and supportive figure in another person.

These kinds of people have the philosophy that "If I'm not with someone, I'm not worthy," "I need another person to feel complete," "Life without the love and attention of another person is not a life," and so on.

○ What Are the Signs That You Are in a Symbiotic Emotional Relationship?

As I've outlined above, a person involved in a symbiotic relationship may feel loved and unique at first, and then a covert depression occurs, although, outwardly, everything is okay. Yet the person is unhappy, lost, feeling that they are losing themselves. Moreover, all social aspects of life are neglected —contact with friends is lost. In a healthy relationship, it is expected that you will share the bulk of your time with your partner and that you will rarely see your friends.

This is a matter of gradually eliminating old friendships while, at the same time, forming new friendships that include your partner. However, in symbiotic relationships, you don't make new friendships, especially not with the opposite sex (e.g., colleague/colleague at work), as these will be misinterpreted. As a result, your social circle shrinks, and you are "doomed" to contact only one person. Personal interests, desires, and goals are reduced or extinguished. In spending more time with your partner, you will neglect your hobbies, interests, activities, and professional development. Even though you realize that something is wrong, you still feel guilty because if they could give up their interests, hobbies, professional challenges, and social circle, how can you not do the same.

Convinced that you have found your true love, you decide to devote yourself entirely to one person because they alone deserve it. A symbiotic relationship is not a healthy relationship between two people. When you assess that you are not progressing with your partner on a personal plane, when you realize that your social life is completely shut down, when you feel unhappy, and depressed, consider whether it is time to change things in your relationship, set boundaries, and fight for your individuality.

CHAPTER 14 - Instructions on How to Manage Codependency

Since codependency is such a long-standing and profound established issue, it frequently takes the assistance of emotional well-being proficient at surviving. These experts can push us to securely investigate the youth issues we have identified with our perspective on connections and recognize the foolish examples that keep us tied to connections that no longer serve us or the excursion we are making.

Suppose you or somebody you know is encountering the signs of a codependent relationship (or character). In that case, it may be an ideal opportunity to converse with somebody, yet nobody, however, the gatherings included, can settle on that choice. Codependency treatment is an incredible asset that centers around helping patients connect with the emotions that they've covered where it counts inside. Yet, they must be available to that work and prepared to roll out the improvements that join it.

How to Avoid Codependent Relationships?

While fixing the many-sided bunches of our mutually dependent hang-ups may be a procedure that requires some serious energy and a clinical expert, avoiding these undesirable relationship designs is not. You can abstain from falling into the snare of a C.D. relationship by knowing the signs early and reaffirming your goals and feeling of self around these five thoughts.

Settle in Vain Not as Much as What You Need *And* What You Merit

Indeed, even in that honeymoon or that exciting period in the wake of making another friend, do not ignore or limit remarks or practices that set you off or cause you to feel "not exactly." Disparaging or ill-bred practices are an admonition sign at any phase in a relationship, and they are an admonition sign that implies STAY CLEAR. Healthy relationships are ones in which we are esteemed for what our identity is —consistently. Thus, in case you are feeling disregarded or excused, leave before you get in too deep.

Decline to Part Away with Yourself

On the off chance that you are somebody who inclines toward "people satisfying" at that point, it is critical to stay cognizant consistently of your inclination to overcompensate. Try not to work more earnestly than you ought to need to intrigue somebody and does not part with yourself in return for being loved or adored. On the off chance that somebody adores you, they will cherish you paying little mind to what your identity is or how you are.

Decline to part with yourself and decline to agree to short of what you merit.

Be Aware of Your Boundaries (And Stick to Them)

Before beginning any new relationship —be it participation or thought— it is fundamental to comprehend your commitments and what their duties are going in. Be as clear as conceivable about your cutoff focuses and encourage them to be clear about theirs as well. You don't owe anybody any bit of your private self. Draw the cutoff lines and stick to them from the crucial ricochet.

Worth Your Body and Your Soul

We live in a culture where sexual contact habitually seems, by all accounts, to be a recreational relaxation action. Yet, it's basic to remember that our bodies are our own and are not owed (in any piece) to the individuals in our lives. Our bodies are not simply our obligations.

They are a vital piece of our breaking point lines. Treat your body as an extension of your soul, and love them both, and you'll see that you can get to a significant setup power in yourself that you didn't' know existed.

Acknowledge and Live Within Your Limitations

While we like to carry on with our lives like we have no restrictions, that simply is not the situation. To maintain a strategic distance from the snare of codependency, it is imperative to acknowledge and live inside our confinements. By doing this, we can evade connections that continually push us to the edge and begin carrying on with a day to day existence that is genuinely our own and loaded up with harmony, light, and euphoria. The key to life is not our romantic relationships or even our friendships — it is figuring out how to live within the lines that genuinely define you.

Assembling All Together…

Codependency is a complex set of practices and convictions that can make it difficult to evade harmful and toxic relationships. The codependent people regularly stick to poisonous and perilous accomplices due to a long rap-sheet of youth injuries that keep them stuck, terrified, and disguising the despicable practices of the individuals around them —making it difficult to just "leave."

Understanding codependency is the best way to recuperate. However, that requires some serious energy, and it frequently takes the assistance of emotional wellness proficient. When we beat our need to, if you do not mind, we can defeat our pasts' agony; however, we need to acknowledge ourselves and our existence fundamentally and unashamedly. Everybody has a past, and everybody has been harmed. The real stunt to life is figuring out how to defeat that hurt to make the presence you have generally merited.

CONCLUSION

Congratulations on making it to the end of this book.

The best known indications of a relationship in a difficult situation are how accomplices differ or fight with each other and how they resolve the dispute between them. Whether they are negative or positive, their goals can affect the tone of the relationship and the way in which confrontations are dealt with. Contradictions that turn into petty quarrels or a constant confrontation on the wire, as a rule, end up in a more uncertain possibility that the relationship will last over time. Fortunately, there are agreements, and resolving conflicts can be moderately simple with the assistance of a specialist. On the off chance that you and your accomplice are not yet and the purpose of seeing a therapist, feeling sympathy without judgment will go a long way in resolving the conflict. It should be possible to tune in and proclaim sympathy by telling your accomplice that you are tuning in. I hope that with this book I have provided you with the information you need to solve your relationship problems.

Good luck!

CPSIA information can be obtained
at www.ICGtesting.com
Printed in the USA
LVHW050748040621
689237LV00005B/263

9 781801 642958